LORE AND LANGUAGE

OF

EARLY EDUCATION

CATHY NUTBROWN

University of Sheffield
Division of Education Publications

ISBN 0 902 831 35 6

University of Sheffield
Division of Education
388 Glossop Road
Sheffield S10 2JA

Publishing imprint: USDE
Series: Papers in Education
Title first published 1998

ISBN 0 902 831 35 6

© C. Nutbrown 1998

Printed by Impact Graphics

Acknowledgements

The author and members of the USDE board thank Professor Tricia David, Canterbury Christchurch College, external referee for this publication .

This publication owes much to the contribution of many colleagues in the Division of Education at the University of Sheffield in particular Ann Clark, Peter Hannon, Gary McCulloch, Elaine Millard, and Jerry Wellington.

The title owes its origins to the work of Iona and Peter Opie and borrows from their book *The Lore and Language of Schoolchildren*, Oxford (1959).

Further information on all the papers in the USDE series is available from:

University of Sheffield
Division of Education
388 Glossop Road
Sheffield S10 2JA

CONTENTS

About the author

Cathy Nutbrown has taught young children and has worked with parents, teachers, nursery nurses and other early childhood educators in a range of group care and education settings. Her research interests include children's early learning and development, their literacy, assessment of learning and work with parents.

For four years (1991-1995), Cathy was Vice President of OMEP (UK) an organisation committed to promoting optimum conditions for children's living and learning; she has represented OMEP UK in several European Countries and the US. She is currently Co-ordinator of the Sheffield University-LEA REAL (Raising Early Achievement in Literacy) Project.

Her publications include *Threads of Thinking – young children learning and the role of early education* (PCP 1994) and *Respectful Educators – Capable Learners* (PCP 1996). The latter's focus on children's rights in early education demonstrates a conviction that young children are entitled to respectful attention in all they do and that their educators must collaborate to examine their work and beliefs in order to ensure that the rights of the youngest children are secured. Her most recent book *Recognising Early Literacy Development – Assessing Children's Achievements* was published in 1997.

FOREWORD

This special paper is one much needed in the field of early childhood education. Cathy Nutbrown pinpoints the ways in which the traditional language of humane, child-centred education has been under attack, ridiculed and treated as outmoded. It has been stealthily replaced by a discourse underpinned by very different values, with the result that the earliest years of childhood are regarded as a mere preparation for later, narrowly defined learning and then work, rather than the Warnock-style education for now and to meet later stages with joy and enthusiasm, ultimately contributing to a 'common good'.

Cathy Nutbrown has selected the key features of this debate and she exposes the weaknesses in the new terminology and its philosophy. At the same time, in her usual, positive manner, Cathy Nutbrown provides alternatives, which in the longer-run are more likely to result in the kind of democratic, cooperative society for which most thinking people expect us to be educating children.

I have no doubt that this will be a popular and key text for those in the field of early years education, because it spells out clearly the anxieties which many practitioners, including those studying for higher degrees, are voicing. The paper is indicating the ways in which we, as a society, risk changing early childhood education to the extent that childhood itself is changed for the worse with the potential future achievements of many of our budding inventors, composers, artists, and thinkers being killed off at this stage.

Tricia David

Professor of Early Childhood Education
Canterbury Christ Church College

OVERVIEW

Early Education in the UK has undergone a period of great change and challenge in the last decade. Largely as a result of Government policy there are problems of: diminishing resources, lack of professional development, an imposed model of school inspection designed for older pupils, an imposed curriculum, and imposed assessment of children as young as four. Increasingly, children are beginning school at four, in large classes, with teachers who have not been trained to teach young children and who lack professional support in their work. There have been perpetual government consultations resulting in detailed documentation which has gradually changed the *language* of early education. As a result, terms which have been used to describe the process of teaching young children are being eliminated in favour of words alien to the *lore* of early education – *play* gives way to *outcomes* and attention to *human interaction* is sidelined to make way for *planned instruction*, in a climate where, paradoxically, what has become traditional practice in early education is often maligned as undesirably progressive.

The Lore and Language of Early Education looks at what early education is for, where it has come from and what has influenced current practice. These three considerations lead on to identification of factors affecting current practice. The *now* is important. It is important for the children, parents and educators who live in the *now*, but as well as an acknowledgement of what is *now*, there must be pioneering for what *will be*. A focus on essentials for effective early education in the coming years concludes this paper.

CENTRAL AIMS OF EARLY EDUCATION

The aims of early education throughout history have been differently expressed, but have grown essentially out of responses to different situations in society at different times. Robert Owen, in establishing his schools in New Lanark in the early 1800s, acted on the need to protect young children from the work place, as well as the value of providing appropriate education for young children whose parents worked in Owen's cotton mills (Lawson and Silver 1973). This early education aimed to attend to the physical and intellectual needs of children, providing a different curriculum and higher level of staffing than the monitorial school system, and space to play and work in small groups, (Owen 1824).

Physical care was a feature of nurseries in the 1920s – with attempts to provide children with fresh air, and hot food, and to instil the virtue of cleanliness. The Macmillan sisters promoted health as well as learning in their open air nurseries, where verandas provided a means of playing and sleeping outdoors. The Rachel McMillan Open Air Nursery School was opened in 1913. The school became the largest and most important in the country built upon the McMillan ideas of early education with large outdoor garden spaces and facilities for children who lived mainly in the slum areas, (Aldrich and Gordon 1989).

Susan Isaacs ran her experimental Malting House School in Cambridge (1924-1927), and contributed to our understanding of children's thinking and learning by writing detailed day-to-day accounts of the things children did and making her analysis of their activities. Isaacs expressed the importance of nursery education:

> 'Much has already been written on the value of the nursery school in providing air and space and exercise, proper rest and good food, and thus remedying the serious lack from which some many children of the nursery age in our large towns suffer. Its function in these respects is well established and widely acknowledged.

> The wider educational work of the nursery school, however, is not yet so generally appreciated. This is true, largely, because our knowledge of the child's feelings and purposes, of his ways of learning and thinking, has itself only recently been known, and is by no means yet complete. We still have much to learn about the child's activities with

different materials and his play with other children at different ages, and the various ways in which we can best foster his mental health. We now do understand something of all this, however, and are beginning to admit its immense importance.'

(Isaacs 1954 p.5)

Isaacs argued that children's minds and bodies could not be considered in isolation and stressed the interrelationship between healthy minds and bodies, referring to children's bodies as instruments of their feelings and intelligence. Susan Isaacs' legacy has encouraged an established practice amongst early educators of observing children and building teaching in ways which matched children's interests and concerns. As the following examples illustrate, an approach to the education of young children which embraced the essentials of life and being part of a wider society, was in accord with the stated aims of Government reports and policies from the 1970s and into the early 1990s.

The Warnock Report of 1978 stated that the aim of education was:

'To enlarge a child's knowledge, experience and imaginative under-standing, and thus his awareness of moral values and capacity for enjoyment; and . . . to enable him to enter the world after formal education is over as an active participant in society and a responsible contributor to it'

Ten years after the Warnock Report, the Education Act (1988) echoed these principles, stating that a broad and balanced curriculum should:

'promote the spiritual, moral, cultural, mental and physical develop-ment of pupils at the school and of society'

and

prepare such pupils for the opportunities, responsibilities and experi-ences of adult life'

(HMSO 1988)

The Select Committee report on Educational Provision for Under Fives (1989) made clear the link between educational achievement and the need to care for children:

The aims for under fives are basically the same as those for any other phase, with the exception that very young children need a considerable additional amount of care. Care and education for the under fives are complementary and inseparable.

(House of Commons ESAC Report 1989)

In 1990, the Committee of Inquiry into the Quality of Educational Experience offered to 3- and 4- year olds stated its agreement with the above select committee statement and emphasised education for the under fives as part of a continuum *'which links home, non-statutory provision and compulsory schooling'.* The Rumbold Committee further considered the central role of parents and the importance of continuity, progression and individual need:

The wide range of developmental stages and needs of very young children puts a great responsibility on educators to provide a curriculum which can take into account the similarities and differences within any group of under fives and also provide continuity with what went before and progression to what will follow. Those responsible for planning the curriculum must also take positive action to ensure that no children are being denied opportunities on account of their race, sex, social background or special needs.

(Rumbold Report 1990 p.8)

In 1990 HMI set out certain principles underlying the education of children under five. These included:

- the crucial role of parents in children's learning
- the need for children to feel secure
- planning and providing for a range of learning needs
- breadth and balance in the curriculum
- purposeful play
- effective use of staff to cater for children's choices and change throughout the day
- assessment to aid planning according to individuals' needs
- equality of opportunity
- a focus on the knowledge, understanding, skills and attitudes in different areas of experience

(HMI 1990 p7-9)

The climate for discussion and development of early education policies seemed to change in the mid 1990s. This can be seen in the 1996 report of the Audit Commission, on the economy, efficiency and effectiveness of under fives provision. The report stated that:

> *Children's early educational experience is crucial for developing the socialisation and learning skills that they will need throughout their lives.*

(Audit Commission 1996. p. 4)

It is worth reflecting on the change here from the language of the Warnock Report (1978) which viewed children as *'active participants' in society* to that of the Audit Commission (1996) which saw early education as a means of *socialisation*.

Though recent Government documentation on nursery education does not state explicitly what nursery education (or different forms of pre-compulsory education) are for, there is a clear emphasis on 'progression':

> *'Children's progress will be at different rates and individual achievement will vary. However, all children should be able to follow a curriculum which enables them to make maximum progress towards the outcomes'*

(DFEE/SCAA 1996 p. 1)

Goals for learning are described as follows:

> *They emphasise early literacy, numeracy and the development of personal and social skills and contribute to children's knowledge, understanding and skills in other areas....they provide a foundation for later achievement.'*

(DFEE/SCAA 1996 p.1)

As the end of the 1990s approached, the clear aim for early education as identified in official documentation seemed to stress future prescribed academic achievement with less value given to the Isaacs' legacy of learning through imagination and individuality. From Robert Owen's New Lanarkshire schools in the early 1800s to the introduction of 'early excellence centres' in the late 1990s there has been an inevitable change in the primary and stated aims of early education. The changing emphasis from physical care and health promotion to academic achievement in some sense marks improved health care and nutrition for children. Those responsible for early education must remain mindful of the need to nurture the emotional and the cognitive, the body and the soul, and in so doing create a form of early education which both challenges and protects young children.

INFLUENCES ON EARLY EDUCATION

The legacy of the 'pioneers' of early education

Much of what is good about the education of young children in the UK, grew out of the work of forward-thinking and intelligent women such as Susan Isaacs and the Macmillan sisters.

Susan Isaacs, writing of her work in the 1920s in the Malting House School, argued for the importance of qualitative records of children – the need for detailed observations of their play and the importance of being clear that an analysis of the learning arising from such play was a distinct adult interpretation of what children actually did. Isaacs explained the importance of qualitative observations of the children at her Malting House School . . .

> The things provided for their use, and the detailed ways in which we responded to their various impulses, led children to be much more generally **active** than they can be under ordinary conditions. This greater activity in all directions, originated, developed and sustained by the children themselves, was a definite part of our educational aim. And it not only led the children to show us their inner minds with far less reserve and fear than in ordinary circumstances, but through the richer, more varied and more immediate experience of the social and physical worlds which it brought to them, it also stimulated and diversified their actual responses. There was, in other words, more for us to see; and we could see it plainly.
>
> (Isaacs 1930 p.12).

The influence of thinkers

The importance of contexts in our understanding of the concepts which interest us has been discussed by Carr (1995) who argues :

> '...in the course of a passage of time, both the meaning of our concepts and our understanding of ourselves may change and become something other than they once were.'

Carr continues

> ...But in neither of these cases is the process of change so complete as to allow either our understanding of a concept or our sense of who we are to become totally detached from their historical roots.'

12

This can be true of educational change. Although it has undergone change, education and its processes are still recognisable as related to education of hundreds of years ago.

> 'Although....the concept of education may now mean something very different to what it meant to past generations, it nevertheless always retains enough of its original meaning to enable us to recognise it as a concept of one and the same thing.'

(Carr, 1995 p 19)

Educational philosophers have influenced pioneers in early education. Mallaguzzi, whose work stimulated the unique and now internationally renowned pre-schools in the Reggio Emilia area of Italy reflected on those who, following Rosa Agazzi and Maria Montessori, influenced his thinking. His list included: Ferrière, Dewey, Vygotsky, Bruner, Piaget, Bronfenbrenner and Hawkins as well as Carr, Kegan, and Gardner, (Edwards, Gandini & Forman 1994). Mallaguzzi's experience illustrates how ideas are garnered from different fields of thinking and interpreted and integrated to make a new and particular philosophy, curriculum and pedagogy.

The 'new pioneers'

Pioneers of nursery education in the UK influenced the development of a form of nursery education which became recognised as amongst the best in the world. But as the visionary Christian Schiller wrote, there is always a need to change:

> Of course there have been great men and women whose vision and action have inspired a generation: Robert Owen, Friedrich Froebel, in our own time Margaret Macmillan, and others. But they pass away, and their ideas pass with them unless these ideas are fashioned into new forms which reflect new circumstances and stand the test of new practices in the contemporary scene. The pioneers take such ideas and refashion and temper them in their daily work in school. Patiently, day after day, week after week and year after year they make the pathway from the past through the present towards the future...

(Schiller 1979)

Early education in the UK must continue to build on good practice and develop the philosophical underpinnings of that practice. In the coming years it must focus on new things too. There are new pioneers of early education, working with and for young children. How they describe and discuss their work will shape the work they do. The language of early education is an integral part of the practice of early education. Articulate discussion is an essential factor in achieving what is good, and can enhance developments by fostering a climate of respect for young children and a belief in nurturing their capability.

FACTORS AFFECTING CURRENT PRACTICE

There are many new pressures on early childhood educators, and – one could argue – on the children they teach. Between 1988 and 1997, in less than a decade, early childhood educators have

- implemented the National Curriculum and subsequent revisions
- faced the introduction of rigorous and stressful inspection processes
- worked with the implementation of the Children Act 1989
- worked to interpret expected 'outcomes' of nursery education
- worked with new codes of practice for the identification of children with Special Educational Needs
- begun to implement changes in relation to National Assessment of children on entry to school
- worked with diminishing resources and increasing expectations
- worked with diminishing support and limited opportunities for professional development
- grappled with issues affecting the teaching of four year olds in school
- worked within a developing network of diversity of provision

Although other sectors of education have also experienced unprecedented change, teachers of the youngest children have been – without respite – at the forefront of educational change. They have witnessed a remoulding of their role, and begun to work in a different educational culture. They have done their utmost to implement national requirements and make them work in the best interests of the children they teach. Progression, progress, and progressive change are positive and bring new freshness. These newnesses belong to the new pioneers, those 'grass roots' educators who see new things in their work – new ways of doing things and new ways of expressing what they do. But change which attempts to move forward by looking selectively and uncritically at the past needs to be met with cautious professionalism.

THE LANGUAGE OF EARLY EDUCATION

A story of language and culture

Once upon a time there was a country called **'Kernow'**; *it was a pretty land – surrounded on three sides by sea. The people spoke their own language, mined the earth, fished the sea and farmed the land. The men lived hard working lives as miners, farmers and fishermen, and the women worked tirelessly too, rearing their children, mending nets, packing herring, working the land. Dolly Pentreath lived in a small Cornish fishing village. She died in 1788 – the last woman to speak Cornish as a first language. On her death a nation – unknowing – began its struggle for survival. The Cornish now strive to maintain their heritage, pass on their traditions and 'ways' to their children, remember 'why' certain things 'are' as they 'are'. Those who invest most effort in the maintenance of Cornish heritage and culture also learn the language – but it is a language that they can only speak with that community made up of others who learn the language in order to preserve it. A handful of Cornish children may know one or two words of their 'mother tongue'. Generation after generation of Cornish children grow up speaking English as their first language and knowing little of their cultural heritage – some may not even know that the Cornish once used a different tongue. The 'Old Cornwall' society preserves much of the County's cultural heritage and language, but Cornish culture is not widespread and there seems a quaintness and novelty value for tourists in things Cornish, rather than a respect for an ancient community and different ways of being.*

Why does this story of the loss of culture in one small English county feature here? Because its message underpins what is to follow. One way to destroy a culture is to attack its language. The destruction of a culture of *Early Education* – intentional or accidental – has been taking place, with fundamental elements of its language being redefined and other elements decried and placed in the same 'wastebasket' category of words and phrases from different cultures and dialects which suggest something less than 'proper'.

The importance of terminology

The words used to describe work with and for young children indicate and influence practice and philosophy in early education. A well rooted and widely understood *language of early education* is necessary for the future development of early education experiences. It is time to consider the terminology used to explain and comment on early education.

Educators, politicians and others use different vocabularies to describe and discuss early education and so convey a variety of assumptions and values. There are positive and negative discourses about children's abilities and struggles in the contexts of their everyday lives. The terminology chosen for each discourse has an impact on what is said or written.

In recent years, a language of battle, managerialism and competition has been composed for education, with terms such as 'orders', 'standards', 'levels', 'stages', 'targets', 'outcomes' and so on. A language more in tune with young children's needs and characteristics includes terms like 'support', 'nurture', 'cherish', 'development', 'facilitation', 'opportunity'. The language and a common understanding of the terms we use are so important. Many early childhood teachers use different vocabularies depending on the context. They read official documentation, record required assessments and communicate in some spheres in the imposed language of the National Curriculum and its assessments. Simultaneously, they may work, think, worry and discuss with colleagues and parents using a language more fitting to cherishing the growth and development of young children.

Conversations that value children's achievements and positive discourses in early childhood are *impossible* without words like development, exploration, facilitation, response, support, interest, investigation and growth, and writings and documents that omit such words should be regarded with suspicion. Early childhood educators must examine the language used to discuss childhood and early education. The terms that are used must be carefully explained so that there can be clear and effective communication between early childhood educators in all sectors, parents, researchers and those who create local and national policy.

Ways in which children and their learning are discussed must be carefully analysed to be sure that new provisions are developed with a clarity of – and fitness for – purpose and with practices which provide children with what they need to learn.

The language we use is crucial. Some changes in early education terminology can mean a loss or devaluing of practices and understanding which feature in the best examples of helping children in their learning.

For example: there are cases where head teachers of nursery schools are now referred to as *'managers'*. The impact is clear; a change of title shifts the nature of the role, and as such changes what is recognised to be important about what head teachers do. The focus moves sharply away from the curriculum and the pedagogical to a language of business and economics.

Other terms suffer from overuse and become devalued through misuse. The currency of the word **quality** has been devalued – quality parenting, quality time, quality environments, quality relationships. Leaflets for parents advertise nurseries which provide "quality" education and care, delivered by "quality" staff. *Quality* is now used so frequently that it has become an almost meaningless prefix.

Structure has always been a term full of difficulty. Some see 'structure' as formal, tight and observable control – whilst many argue that the best structures in early childhood are those which are fluid and which allow for individuality and creativity. Fluidity of learning opportunities allows children's brains to structure themselves – those myriad connections growing as one brain connects with another and children form new thoughts, new ideas, and new knowing. Manning and Sharp (1973) provided a framework within which to structure children's play through the pioneering (and hitherto unsurpassed) Schools' Council 'Structuring Play' Project. Teachers who embarked on a structuring play course developed clear and workable understandings of what it meant to 'structure' children's play and the dynamism resulting from this work in nurseries and infant classrooms bore witness to the impact of sustained and supported professional development for teachers, which made teachers think and in turn challenged children to think and learn.

Some early childhood organisations have changed their terms too. For example the former Pre-school Playgroups Association deleted the word *play* and renamed the organisation. In speculating on the reasons for this there are questions which could be asked. Did play suddenly become unrespectable? No one would deny that *'learning'* is important, but since the work of the Macmillans and Isaacs, the *process of play* with *learning* being an outcome of play, has been an acknowledged essential of early education. Is it now the case that the identifiable learning outcome is more important than the process? Have statements of the specific assumed importance over the development of transferable skills for finding out and learning other new things? Perhaps it was believed that the term play was becoming misunderstood – as in *they just play*. If that was the case – if that *is* the case – excluding one of the most important words for describing children's active learning and one of the roots of early education exacerbates rather than eliminates the problem. A better solution is to define what early educators mean when they talk about *play*. Play needs to be defined in ways which ensure that everyone with an interest in or responsibility for the education of young children under-stands what is meant. It has been stated that *outcomes* – what is actually learned – are more desirable than the *process* of learning. It cannot be denied that what comes out of the process of learning is important. However, all who learn, at whatever age, can comment for themselves on the importance of the *processes* of learning and of teaching and the impact of those processes on what is learned and on *motivation* and *satisfaction*.

Whose language?

Whose language is being spoken when early education is discussed? Is it a language which has developed through many decades of thought and debate and which is understood by parents and professionals who work with children, or an imposed *'standard speak'* with which educators collude because they see no alternative – or (worse) because they have not noticed the change?

In its report *'Counting to Five'*, the Audit Commission (1996) highlighted three words which it used to describe key factors in under fives provision – *economy, efficiency, effectiveness*. To what extent do these terms – more suited to the Harvard Business School than to early childhood settings – describe philosophy and practice in work with young children? They may well indicate the current political and social climate, but *economy, efficiency, effectiveness* must be balanced with other things if children in future years are to receive the early education they are entitled to. It is worth considering new terms for early education: *rights, responsibilities, re-creation,* and *reaching for the stars*.

New terms for early education

If early education in the coming decades is to serve the needs of children as well as meet the aims of governments, there are some essentials which need to be considered. There must be a serious consideration of children's rights and of adults' responsibilities. There must be an approach to teaching young children which includes re-creation and recreation and one which offers challenge to the point where children reach for the stars in their learning and achievement.

Children's rights

An understanding of and commitment to recognising and respecting children's rights and a re-examination of early education practice in terms of children's rights is urgently needed (Nutbrown 1996). Everyone who is serious about work with and for children could seek to improve their practice by considering what boundaries to children's rights exist in their encounters with children. As policies and practices are considered the question to be asked is: *What stands in the way of children's rights?*

There is work to do in helping *children* to learn about their rights, and in helping *educators* to learn about children's rights. The writings of children from Reggio Emilia, (Reggio Children 1995), indicate that their educators have explored ways of helping *children* to think about their rights, as well as striving to fulfil the UN Convention, (United Nations 1989), through their policies and practices.

The early 1990s witnessed a perpetual tension in Britain about day care and education for our youngest children. Cases have been made about different kinds of provision. Voluntary run playgroups argued that they were best placed to provide for the non-statutory age group; private nurseries grew and promoted themselves as the most flexible service for working parents; state nursery classes and nursery schools continued to assert that they offered the most appropriate kind of curriculum, built on a tradition of good practice and linked into the later educational expectations of the National Curriculum; childminders stated that they offered the most personal and responsive service to parents. Tensions and rivalries involved voluntary, private and state providers.

There was an unfortunate subtext to this situation driven by financial concerns, around issues like which service was 'best' and which should therefore receive Government funding and endorsement. The Early Childhood Education Forum was formed amidst this debate, under the umbrella of the National Children's Bureau and chaired by Gillian Pugh. This was an attempt to find common ground from which to take forward the case for quality in early childhood education, whatever the setting. Speculation was rife throughout 1994 and early 1995 whilst the

Government appeared to ponder on its policy and its commitment to under fives provision. In July 1995 a decision to provide parents of 4 year-old children with a voucher with which they could purchase some form of 'education' was announced. Consultation documents on *Desirable Outcomes for Children's Learning*, the *'Light touch' Inspection*, and the *Voucher* system of funding 'education' for four year olds, were issued in September 1995, (SCAA 1995, DFEE/DOH 1995, DFEE 1995) Within this climate, various claims and counter claims were being made about the different types of provision. There was discussion about the immediate benefits, long term benefits and uppermost in the minds of those who watch the purse strings was the term 'value for money'. The Audit Commission for England and Wales carried out a study into nursery education (1994-1995) and examined different types of provision in order to study, among other things: resources; local authority strategy; the length of time children spend in each setting; and assessment of effectiveness of different experiences and types of experiences. The principal objective was to consider how to make the best use of resources rather than to recommend what the overall level of provision should be or what constituted 'good' or 'bad' practice (Audit Commission 1996).

A climate of competition rather than collaboration existed between providers and advocates of particular types of provision and, at times, gave the feeling that organisations and agencies were existing to perpetuate their own existence rather than further the cause for which they were first established – namely to provide opportunities for young children to play and learn. There were vast differences in inspections of provision for under fives, with LEA nursery schools and classes being inspected by the rigour of OFSTED inspection every four years and playgroups, crèches, private nurseries and childminders having to comply with a more health and safety oriented inspections required in the Children Act 1989, (Ensing 1996, Pugh 1992). The qualifications and experience of OFSTED and Children Act inspectors vary tremendously, as do the criteria for inspection and the detail of the reports. Moves in 1995 to 'marry' OFSTED and Children Act inspections were welcomed from the point of view of sensibility, but there were some worries that the rigour of inspections of nursery schools and classes may be lost. If they were inspected by different criteria and processes, the status of their inspections could be reduced, they might be marginalised from other forms of education in the school system and the development of positive experiences for young children could be threatened in a watering down or levelling out of all forms of 'under fives' provision rather than achieving excellence in provision across the spectrum (Ensing 1996). Those plans did not come to fruition, and two inspection systems remain with *Desirable Outcomes* as a focus in both inspection regimes.

The jumble of provision gives the illusion of choice and diversity, but in reality presents an unhelpful situation for parents making decisions about forms of early education and care, and masks the reality of a lack of provision. So how might parents and early childhood educators make decisions about quality of provision?

One way of deciding whether provision is 'good enough' for children whatever the label might be, is to examine it in terms of children's rights, (Nutbrown 1996). Although currently such issues are not overtly included in inspection criteria for day care or education settings in the UK, for any provision to be 'good enough for children', parents, policy makers, educators and children must have confidence in it. Early childhood provision must be good enough for what could be termed the 'Confident Mark'. To achieve a state where provision for children receives such recognition, educators and policy makers must embrace the rights of the child. Children's Rights, are the responsibility of everyone, not simply of the Government of the day. Every educator, indeed every adult citizen, must come to realise that they, as well as Government, have a responsibility to work for children's rights and that they can do much on a day to day basis to support, extend and uphold children's rights. The signalled intention of the Government in 1997 to incorporate the European Convention on Human Rights into UK domestic law was welcomed, along with warnings that all the Principles of the UN Convention on the Rights of the Child still need to be implemented and should not be overshadowed by the move on Human Rights, (Gunner 1997).

In addition to the rights of children enshrined in the UN Convention, early education could consider four more rights for children:

The Right to Opportunities
Children need opportunities to explore, express, discover, create, solve, resolve, challenge, explain, ask, listen . . .

> **Early education must create accessible opportunities
> and provide 'essential opportunities'**

This has implications for resources – human and material. Issues to consider include:

- appropriately qualified and experienced people
- properly planned and constructed buildings
- sufficient and appropriate equipment
- services which acknowledge that children are individuals

> **Opportunities for children include enhanced professional
> development for their educators and respectful assessment
> of their learning and their needs.**

The Right to Recognition

How can educators ensure that the effort of *all* children is recognised? Children need adults who understand their learning and are insightful enough to try – respectfully – to show recognition of children's efforts and achievements, and to celebrate the successes that children themselves identify as the following example shows:

> Two and a half year old Alex persisted in putting a nursery rhyme tape into the tape player herself. Attempts by adults to help were loudly resisted. 'No I do it myself' she shouted. She had several near misses but eventually she managed successfully to insert the tape and set it going. 'I did it – did it – did it myself ', she shouted. And having done so she stopped the tape playing – took it out and repeated the successful manoeuvre. Adults watching realised that their role was to recognise and celebrate Alex's success at her chosen goal – not to insist that they then listened to the tape – nor to discourage her from 'playing' with the tape machine. Listening has ceased to be the objective – operating the technology was her focus now.

> Recognition means acknowledgement of children's chosen goals and of their achievements as well as their needs and a readiness to admit to their humanity, their tenacity, their rights, their language, their culture, their learning and their love.

The Right to Interaction

> **Adult knowledge of children's thinking is essential to enhanced interaction in learning.**

Children need to spend their time with adults who respond to them and interact with them in ways which capture their interest, preserve their vitality and take them further into learning. Adults need to find ways of using their expertise to interact appropriately and their humanity to interact responsively and reciprocally, as in the following extract from *Threads of Thinking* (Nutbrown 1994).

This transcript contains the story which one little girl had to tell. Starting from her interest in a particular illustration in Shirley Hughes' *Up and Up*, she builds on her ideas about life and her own experiences. The adult tries throughout to reflect the child's own language and ideas back to her without asking new questions or imposing her own 'adult' agenda:

Lucy	*She's going up, right up to the roof.*
Teacher	*She's up on top of the roof, she's getting higher.*
Lucy	*I think she might be in Heaven soon.*
Teacher	*You think she might be in Heaven?*
Lucy	*Well she's nearly high enough to be in Heaven, that's why the people are chasing her.*
Teacher	*The people are chasing her because they think she's getting as high as Heaven?*
Lucy	*Yes, as high as Heaven, they don't want her to go as high as that!*

Teacher	*They don't want her to go as high as Heaven?*
Lucy	*If you go as high as Heaven you get stuck and can't get down. You can get up there but you can't get back. My rabbit did that. Aeroplanes go high but not as high as Heaven, so they're OK. I went to my holiday in an aeroplane, but it wasn't in Heaven. I went for a long time though.*

(Nutbrown, 1994 pp.105-106)

The reflective language of the teacher enabled Lucy to tell the story she had formed within her. It illustrates the way she has, at the age of 4 years, begun to understand about death and parting. She has taken the explanation that her rabbit has 'gone to Heaven' and attached to it her own meaning. To her, going to Heaven is not about death, but it *is* about parting, because that beloved rabbit is now stuck in a place and unable to get back to her. The teacher enabled the story, not by asking 'why' or 'how' or by adding in ideas of her own, but by creating a space in which Lucy could tell her own story and know she would be heard. Ways in which adults can take time to interact with children, creating space for them as well as challenging them, deserve the fullest attention.

The Right to Adult Models

> **Children need models from whom to learn. They learn much from what they see and are quick to take on attitudes and mannerisms, attitudes and values of adults around them.**

Children need adults who, through their actions and words, support the development of their positive self esteem, models who show children the need to explore and find out and question. Children need models who demonstrate their own interest in knowing and doing, who show that it is legitimate and appropriate to ask for help. Children need to see adults sticking at a challenge until it is complete. Adults need to convey to children that even they find some learning difficult. Young children need adults who show them the importance of co-operation not conflict, and who demonstrate respect for others through their most human interactions.

25

Children will attend to the behaviour of adults they live with, adults who work with them, and adults in a wider context of society. The behaviour of adults they see in the media and the models of caring and living and learning that are perpetuated in society are powerful models for young children – all adults have responsibilities in this area of children's lives. Children have a right to adult models to help their learning. Learning about, learning with and learning for.....Children's rights are adults' responsibilities (Nutbrown 1996).

Adults' responsibilities

Children's rights cannot be realised unless and until adults accept that they all have a responsibility *towards* children and power they can use *for* them. The nature of the responsibilities may differ but parents, educators, researchers, administrators, business personnel, and politicians all have responsibilities towards children and the world in which they live and learn. That responsibility will take many forms – staying informed, deciding how to vote, writing to our MPs, researching and disseminating key issues, considering and acting on environmental and global issues, as will the responsibilities of those who interact with children on a regular basis. Adults responsibilities also include creating learning environments, the physical surroundings and emotional climates in which children are 'disposed to learn'.

In nurseries across the UK, there are fresh examples daily of what can be accomplished when adults turn responsibility from the rhetoric of policy into the reality of practice. Equally, it will be possible to find situations where the converse is true, where policy and practice are divorced and where children do not always reap the benefits of working alongside adults who take their responsibility seriously.

It is adults' responsibility to nurture children to be responsible – to themselves, to others and to their environments.

Re-creation

Some say that children do not need to re-invent the wheel – they simply need an older generation to tell them. But many adults still learn best when they do something for themselves. One generation cannot simply pass on information to the next. Of course there is much that teachers can teach children, but they can also *help children to learn* many other things.

Children re-create as children learn. They re-create the forms of people as they *discover* how they can draw the likenesses of people they know and places they visit, the ideas of their dreams. They re-create stories, re-moulding stories first told to them, making them their own. Unaware of history or traditions children *discover* nursery rhymes for themselves, repeat them and re-compose them, and in the process build a fundamental cornerstone of reading. Children do not simply recite nursery rhymes – they take *ownership* of them, make them anew, for themselves. When a child makes her first sand castle it is the first sand castle that has ever been made – new, fresh, original. Re-creation is an essential part of being human and an indispensable key to human learning.

Recreation too is essential for balance in life – as Robert Fulghum advises:

> *Live a balanced life – learn some, and think some, and draw and paint and sing and dance and play and work – every day – some.*

(Fulghum 1990)

Reaching for the stars

Effective early education is about emotion as well as cognition – feeling as well as thinking and doing. It means supporting children in achieving their daily goals. *Reaching for the stars* means exploring the emotions of wonder as well as the intricacies of technology. In their own ways and using all of their abilities and understandings children are re-creating the world – contemplating the stuff of the world, grappling with the kinds of questions that challenge scientists and mathematicians, and in the process they are *reaching for more stars of learning* about the world and their place in it.

Children *reach for the stars* in their questions too – striving and struggling to make sense of their world.

The four year old who asks : *Why are there trees?*

The three year old who asked : *Why does the sea go in and out?*

The two year old who asked her mother: *What does the moon do and where does the sun go?*

The one year old who finds a collection of pine cones in a basket and seemingly ponders to himself *What can I do with these?*

The six month old who holds and sucks and stares at a cool round shell in her hand – perhaps asking *what is this that I have here?*

Reaching for the stars in early education means challenging children to aim for their potential and to express their dreams.

NEW COMPONENTS OF EARLY EDUCATION FOR THE FUTURE

Three key areas need attention in order to realise children's rights, adults' responsibilities, to encourage children's re-creation and recreation and to enable children to reach for the stars in their learning:

- *children's rights*
- *respectful assessment*
- *professional development*

Children's rights

In December 1991, the UK government ratified the UN Convention on the Rights of the Child. It addressed children's rights to protection, freedom from discrimination, survival and development, security in family life and the right to participate in matters concerning them. Three years later in the first UK Government report on progress on implementation, there was a failure to acknowledge any need to change, improve, reconsider, monitor or resource any legislation, policy, practice, (Lansdown 1996 p.2) A non-governmental report from the UK Children's Rights Development Unit (Lansdown and Newell 1994) offered the UN Committee a more critical analysis of the UK implementation of the Convention, which prompted criticism of many aspects of government policy both in relation to the rights contained in the Convention and the lack of procedures in place to implement the Convention in the UK.

Those who argue against children's rights sometimes do so on the basis that rights mean responsibility and children should not be burdened with responsibility. But for little children, adults must recognise children's rights whilst taking for them the burden of responsibility, (just as they take responsibility for feeding them, clothing them, and keeping them safe until they are able to be responsible for their own well-being).

Lansdown writes:

> *The Convention provides the basic tools for analysing and evaluating practice. The task is now in the hands of every adult living or working with children to translate those tools into fundamental changes in the reality of children's lives.*

> (Lansdown 1996 p.10)

The roles and responsibilities of educators in terms of children's rights are explored more fully in *Respectful educators – Capable learners* (Nutbrown ed. 1996).

Respectful Assessment

In the coming years we need a change in assessment – both of children and of provision. Despite a multitude of assessment instruments, assessment of young children's learning is still problematic (Nutbrown 1997) and assessment of provision remains in need of improvement and refinement (Ensing 1996).

Rights and responsibilities in assessment of children

Adults have clear and serious responsibilities in terms of assessment, and in carrying out those responsibilities, they are charged with respecting children's rights to 'respectful assessment'. Those who devise assessment processes and those who carry out assessments must not underestimate, misuse or abuse their power.

Issues of 'rights' and 'responsibilities' are fundamental to this discussion of assessment. According to the UN Convention on the Rights of the Child adopted by the General Assembly of the United Nations on 20 November 1989, ratified by the UK government in December 1991, children have a right to be taught according to their need and in ways which enable them to reach their potential. Teaching that enables children to reach their potential requires good assessment processes.

Assessment of a learner's present knowing is a sound basis upon which to base the next teaching plans. The development, implementation and evaluation of effective assessment in the classroom is the responsibility of the adults who work with and for children and education, including: teachers, researchers and policy makers. In terms of assessing early development it is therefore a case of children's rights and adults' responsibilities.

Mary Jane Drummond wrote of the assessment of children's learning in terms of rights, responsibilities and power (Drummond 1993). She recalls the work of a group of teachers on an Educational Studies course who were engaged in an exercise to identify their responsibilities to their pupils. Having identified their responsibility, the teachers identified another imperative:

> *...which would be needed to complement the concept of responsibility: the need to affirm our ability to meet our responsibilities to the height of our professional powers.*

(Drummond 1993 p.169)

The power of assessors can be infinite and ultimate. In educational assessment, from a beginning in the pre-school period to the highest academic qualifications, assessors and systems have power over those who are being assessed. From assessments of the pre-school child to the PhD candidate, systems and assessors must show respect for learners – to the extent that they acknowledge and use their power with respect for what others know and with a disposition to appreciate when they themselves have more to learn. Children have the right to respectful assessment and adults have the responsibility to provide it. The expertise of the educator is a crucial part of that responsibility:

> *Adult knowledge is crucial to extending children's learning and essential if children's early achievements are to be recognised and respected.*

(Nutbrown 1996 p 54)

The concept of 'respectful assessment' is used to include a variety of assessment approaches that fit the purpose:

> *Respectful assessment takes account of a range of factors and achievements, values the participation of the person being assessed as well as the perspectives of those carrying out the assessment. It includes self-assessment and collaborative assessment as well as assessment of one person by someone else.*

(Nutbrown 1996 p 52)

Unfortunately, the Chief Inspector of Schools considered this way of describing assessment an 'impossible ideal' (Woodhead 1997). This makes it all the more important for teachers and researchers to take account of the rights of learners and to use their responsibilities with respect. If the power of those involved in developing, administering and reporting assessments is denied, there remains the danger that assessment processes will ride roughshod over children's learning and development, and in so doing, miss much of what children can do.

Many existing forms of assessment are inadequate and the challenge is to adopt assessment practices that:

- value early achievements
- respect the ways in which learning develops
- involve parents
- acknowledge the rights of children to respectful assessment
- acknowledge the respective responsibilities of researchers, educators, and policy makers in the implementation of such assessments
- do not abuse children by misuse of the power held by assessors or those who devise assessment tools.

Issues of early assessment are not solely the domain of professionals. They are the concern of parents too – the people from whom young children learn much in the pre-school years. Parents have a distinct contribution to make to the assessment of children's early learning and some instruments have been successful in including parents in assessment.

The School Curriculum and Assessment Authority (1996) described parental involvement as a feature of good practice. With particular reference to assessment it identified good practice taking place when:

> Children's progress and future learning needs are assessed and recorded through frequent observation and are shared regularly with parents.
>
> (SCAA 1996 p.6)

But professionals *sharing* what they have noticed with parents is only part of the picture. For example: Parents know much about their children's literacy learning and many parents are in a position to give teachers extra insights into their children's early literacy, such as :

- the books they most enjoy
- the environmental print they recognise
- the writing events they share in and often initiate at home
- the rhymes they know well.

The *REAL* (Raising Early Achievement in Literacy) Project has developed four developmental jigsaws which help parents to identify the elements of literacy that their children are involved in and use at home (Nutbrown and Hannon 1997). These jigsaws, focusing on four strands of literacy development: environmental print, books, writing and key aspects of oral language, locate assessment of early literacy development with children's parents and put them in the position of sharing what they know with their child's teachers.

Ongoing assessment for the purposes of teaching and learning is incomplete without some contribution from parents. What children do in an educational setting is only part of their profile – just as a formal assessment can only provide a part of the picture. Home learning, as observed by parents, can give teachers and other early childhood educators a clearer, more holistic image of a child's all round literacy development.

Much of what young children do and learn is of such importance and complexity that it is quite immeasurable – but nevertheless remarkable and worthy of recognition.

Respectful assessment of provision.....

The desirable learning outcomes are likely to be met for personal and social development and physical development. Language and literacy and mathematics are generally satisfactory with a few weaknesses in both areas. Knowledge and understanding of the world is unlikely to be fostered at the moment as this area has many weaknesses. Creative work is varied but has some weaknesses.

(from a Nursery Education Inspection Report 1997)

One has to ask whether such a summary is respectful of those inspected, those reading the report and indeed of the inspector, required to write in such a style. Simply to list weaknesses in such a summary form is an unhelpful beginning to a report which concluded that, despite more weaknesses than strengths,

Taken overall, the quality and standards of the educational provision are acceptable in promoting the desirable outcomes for children's learning.....

More respectful *systems* of inspecting provision, both of the range of pre-school provision and of schools are required. The form of OFSTED inspections which causes great stress to staff of a school cannot be as respectful as it might be. It leaves many teachers exhausted and as such less able to inject energy into their teaching in the weeks following an inspection.

Inspection reports, be they for registration of Under 8's provision or OFSTED inspection of schools, could be more respectful in the *language* they use – of those who are assessed and those who attempt to read, understand and learn the full meaning and implications of the reports.

Assessment of children and of provision for learning which highlights needs and difficulties as well as strengths and achievements, is an essential component in teaching and learning. Even the most difficult assessments which highlight many inadequacies in provision can be carried out with respect for the people involved and for the children who attend.

Professional development

'Professional development' provides much wider, democratic and far reaching opportunities for early childhood educators to learn than does 'training'. It involves reading, shared experiences, stimulating thought, the development of new ideas and practice, in addition to reflection and evaluation. 'Training' is a term that represents one narrow part of learning 'how to do something' – complete a particular form, carry out a particular kind of assessment – in short how to follow procedures. Some 'training' is needed, but it is not sufficient alone to support early childhood educators in fulfilling their role and enabling them in their turn, to support and uphold children's rights, understand and fulfil their own responsibilities, facilitate children as they re-create and in their recreation, and encourage children to reach for the stars of learning. It is fair to say that since the 1988 Education Act teachers have had too much training and too few professional development opportunities.

A new dimension must be added to the learning opportunities that are offered to those who work with young children. It is not good enough simply to change the label and call all training 'professional development'. The content must be examined and a clear decision made about what is offered to early childhood educators. If we want young children to think, we need to provide challenging opportunities for their educators to think too. Children in early education need professionals who know *why* they do *what* they do. They need adults who reflect on what has happened – who evaluate their practice and who look forward to the next step in improving their responses to children's needs.

CONCLUSION

Respect and capability

When advocates of respect for children are accused of being 'idealistic', of 'romanticising early childhood', their meaning is misunderstood. Respect is not about 'being nice' – it is about being clear, honest, courteous, diligent and consistent. *Respect* for children's rights is a disposition that can nurture the capabilities in young children. *Respect* for children will enable adults (early childhood educators, parents, researchers, HMI, Government ministers, policy makers), to fulfil their responsibilities towards children. *Respect* for children is a disposition which enables adults who work with young children to fulfil their responsibilities, enabling re-creation where children discover and make and play and grow. *Respect* for young children gives educators the courage to assert that they want the kind of early education for all our young children which enables them to *'reach for the stars'* of learning while they still believe in the magic of the moon.

REFERENCES

ALDRICH, R. and GORDON, P. (1989) *Dictionary of British Educationists* London: Woburn Press

AUDIT COMMISSION (1996) *Counting to Five – education of children under five* London: HMSO

CARR, W. (1995) *For Education – towards critical educational inquiry* Buckingham: Open University Press

COMMITTEE OF INQUIRY INTO THE QUALITY OF EDUCATIONAL EXPERIENCE OFFERED TO 3- AND 4- YEAR OLDS (1990) *Starting with Quality* (Rumbold Report) London: HMSO

DES (1990) *The Education of Children Under Five* London: HMSO

DFEE/SCAA (1996) *Desirable Outcomes of Nursery Education on Entry to Compulsory Schooling* London: SCAA

DRUMMOND, M.J. (1993) *Assessing Children's Learning* London: David Fulton

EDWARDS, C., GANDINI, L. and FORMAN, G. (1994) *The Hundred Languages of Children The Reggio Emilia Approach to Early Childhood Education* Norwood, N.J: Ablex Publishing

ENSING, J. (1996) Inspection of Early Years in School. In Nutbrown (1996) *Respectful Educators – Capable Learners: children's rights in early education* London: Paul Chapman Publishing

FULGHUM, R. (1990) *All I really need to know I learned in kindergarten* New York: Villard Books

GUNNER, A. (1997) Children's rights = human rights? *Children UK* 15 Winter 1997 pp12-13

HMSO (1988) *Education Reform Act* Part 1 chapter 1(2) London: HMSO

HOUSE OF COMMONS EDUCATION, SCIENCE AND ARTS COMMITTEE: (1989) *Educational Provision for the Under Fives* London: HMSO

ISAACS, S. (1930) *Intellectual Growth in Young Children* London: Routledge & Kegan Paul

ISAACS, S. (1954) *The Educational Value of the Nursery School* London: British Association for Early Childhood Education

LANSDOWN, G. (1996) The United Nations Convention on the Rights of the Child – Progress in the United Kingdom. In Nutbrown (1996) *Respectful Educators – Capable Learners: children's rights in early education* London: Paul Chapman Publishing

LANSDOWN, G. & NEWELL, P. (1994) *Agenda for Children* London: Children's Rights Development Unit

LAWSON, J. and SILVER, H. (1973) *A Social History of Education in England* London: Methuen

MANNING, K. and SHARP, A. (1973) *Structuring Play in the Early Years of School* London: Schools Council

NUTBROWN, C. and HANNON, P. (1997) *Preparing for Early Literacy Education with Parents, a professional development manual* Nottingham: NES-Arnold/REAL Project

NUTBROWN, C. (1994) *Threads of Thinking – young children learning and the role of early education* London: Paul Chapman Publishing

NUTBROWN, C. (1996) *Respectful Educators – Capable Learners: children's rights and early education* London: Paul Chapman Publishing

OWEN, R. An outline of the system at New Lanark (Glasgow 1824) pp 32-3 – Select Committee on Education of the Lower Orders of the Metropolis (London 1816; 1968 edition)

REGGIO CHILDREN (1995) *A Journey into the Rights of Children – as seen by the children themselves* Italy: Municipality of Reggio Emilia – Infant - Toddler Centres and Pre-schools

REPORT OF THE COMMITTEE OF ENQUIRY INTO SPECIAL EDUCA-TIONAL NEEDS (Warnock Committee) (1978) London: HMSO

SCHILLER C. (1979) *Christian Schiller in his Own Words* London: National Association for Primary Education/A&C Black Ltd.

UNITED NATIONS (1989) *Convention on the Rights of the Child* New York: United Nations

WOODHEAD, C. (1997) Do we have the schools we deserve? Annual Lecture by Chris Woodhead, Her Majesty's Chief Inspector of Schools in England, Tuesday 25 February 1997 London

INDEX